Animal Talk

Lisa Thompson

sundance
A Haights Cross Communications Company

A Haights Cross Communications Company

Copyright © 2003 Sundance Publishing

This edition of The Real Deal is published
by arrangement with Blake Education.
All rights reserved. No part of this publication
may be reproduced or transmitted in any form
or by any means, electronic or mechanical,
including photocopy, recording, or any
information or retrieval system, without
permission in writing from the publisher.

Published by
Sundance Publishing
P.O. Box 740
One Beeman Road
Northborough, MA 01532–0740
800-343-8204
www.sundancepub.com

Copyright © text Lisa Thompson
Copyright © illustrations Alex Frank, Luke Jurevicius, and Cliff Watt

First published 2002 by
Blake Education, Locked Bag 2022, Glebe 2037, Australia
Exclusive United States Distribution: Sundance Publishing

Design by Cliff Watt in association with
Sundance Publishing

Animal Talk
ISBN 0-7608-6683-X

Photo Credit
p. 9 (bottom right) Michael Curtain

Printed in Canada

Table
of Contents

Dog Speak

**Dogs don't use words,
but they are great talkers.**

Dogs bark, howl, grunt, growl, and whine.
It's not a good idea to use these noises
when talking to a dog. If you don't get it
right, the dog won't understand a word
you are saying!

Crazy human.

From Wolf to Woof

Dogs are distantly related to wolves. Like wolves in a **pack,** dogs rank themselves when they get together. The strongest dog will lift its head highest and point its tail up.

OK, OK! You're the boss!

Coyotes

It may put its head or paw on another dog's shoulder. Or it may even hold the other dog's **muzzle** in its mouth, like the coyote below. This means, "I'm the boss!"

Not all dogs want to be top dog. When a dog knows that it is weaker, it will lower its head or roll over and show its belly. That's dog talk for, "I surrender" or "You are my leader."

Q: How do you find a lost dog in the woods?
A: *Put your ear next to a tree and listen for the bark.*

7

Nosing Around

Dogs say hello by sniffing each other. Sniffing is also how dogs pick up the daily news. Dogs have an amazing sense of smell—about 100,000 times better than yours. Just by smelling a tree, a dog can tell which dog has been there, what it had for dinner, and what its mood was.

A dog's nose also knows how you are feeling. People give off different **scents** when they are in different moods. One sniff, and a dog can tell if you are angry or if you want to play.

I can smell my squeak toy!

I can smell a dead mouse a block away!

What's your smell IQ?

The amount of lining in a dog's nose helps it to smell things people could never smell.

PEOPLE

 3 square centimeters

DOGS

up to 150 square centimeters

Face Facts

"I'm happy!"

"I'm confused."

"Let me check this out."

"I'm angry!"

The Dog's Body Language Guide

When you learn dog language, you may be surprised by what a dog says—and by how a dog says it! Almost every part of a dog's body carries a message. Here's a quick guide.

One ear up means, "I'm on the lookout!"

Dogs like to lift their nose higher than another dog's nose. It says, "I am the top dog!"

A dog raises its paw, lifts its nose, and pricks up its ears when it smells danger.

Dear Dr. Paws,
My dog jumps on
one foot and twists
up and down.

Confused

Dear Confused,
Don't worry.
Your dog is
just *"going for a spin,"* a
popular doggie dance.

Dr. Paws

Ears back and down mean, "I'm worried."

Some dogs raise their hair in anger or fear.

A loose, swaying body means, "I'm happy!"

A stiff body means, "Danger! Back off!"

Tail Talk

"I'm happy!"

"I'm feeling sad."

"I'm relaxed and feeling good."

"Danger!"
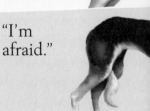

"I'm afraid."

"You're the boss."

Cat Chat

Imagine waking up to find a freshly killed mouse on your pillow!

Mother cats bring home dead mice. It teaches kittens that mice are good to eat. Cats also think of people as their kittens. So when a cat brings you a dead mouse, it is trying to feed you! Cats must be very confused by your reaction!

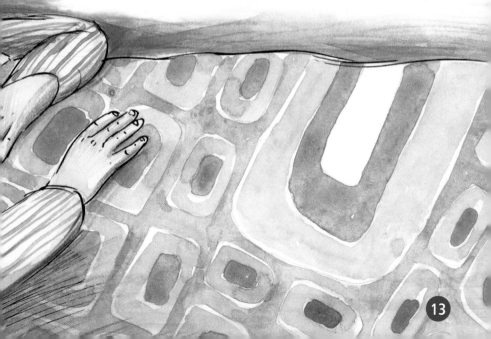

Butting In

A newspaper! I think I'll butt in.

If a cat really likes you, it will say hello with a head butt! This is the same way kittens speak to their mother. Cats have small scent **glands** on their faces. When a cat rubs its face against you, it mixes its scent with yours. You can't smell it, but you are now marked as part of the cat's family!

Tail Talk

Here's how to read a cat's tail.

Description	What it means
Tail hanging down and loose.	"Everything is OK."
Tail straight up with the tip bent over.	"I'm not sure. Let me check you out."
Hair standing up on body and tail; back arched.	"I'm dangerous! Look out!"

Cat Calls

Scientists have found that cats can make at least 20 different sounds. They may hiss, scream, or yowl depending on what is happening. But most of the time, one sound—meow—says it all. A cat's meow can mean many different things. It all depends on tone and volume.

Cats also purr—a sound that no other animal can make. Kittens only a week old first purr to tell their mother that they are OK. Cats purr when they are feeling social. They purr when they are happy, but also when they are in pain.

Q: What happened to the cat that ate a lemon?

A: *It turned into a sour puss!*

MEOW MEOW
MEOW MEOW
MEOW MEOW
MEOW MEOW

Purrrrrrrr

MEEEE-OOO-WWW

This means the cat wants your attention.

MYUP!

Cats use this to say, "Ouch!" Did you stand on their paw or tail?

MIEEEEEOOORRRRWWW

Said by a cat when it really likes something.

MEROW!

"Back off!" Don't go near this cat!

REEEEEE-OOWWWW-RR-YOWW

Screams and growls often mean a cat is afraid and trying to scare an enemy.

On the Prowl

Hunting comes naturally to cats. They are born with the **instinct** to chase anything that moves quickly. Tie a piece of paper to a long length of string. Drag the paper on the ground in front of the cat. Watch the cat's body language as it crouches and gets ready to pounce. Perhaps the cat is also saying, "I'm alert!" by twitching the tip of its tail. Get ready for the attack! It's just like a cat in the wild.

Cheetah

THE CAT'S GUIDE TO LIFE
If another cat invades your territory,
do the cat STARE!

1
Sit. Tuck your paws under your chest. Pull in your neck. This makes you look bigger and scarier.

Fluff up hair

Make tail bigger

Pump up chest

2
Stare and look away.

Looking the other way is good for cross-eyed cats

What the leg looks like under the fur

Make sure the back legs are ready for a fast getaway

3
Continue staring until the other cat leaves or starts a fight.

Make eyes big

Alert ears

No blinking!

Keep whiskers up!

Wild Animals Talk, Too

You might not even notice animals in the wild communicating—but their lives often depend on getting the message right!

A male black widow spider walks carefully across a female's web. As it walks, it tugs a signal on the web: "I'm not an enemy! Don't eat me!" One wrong tug and the male might end up as dinner.

It's All in the Moves!

If you want to understand animals in the wild, you'll need to watch them closely. Just as with dogs, cats, and humans, body language can say a lot. Take a look at how these animals use posture, movement, and facial expression to get their message across.

I'm really angry!

23

Doing the Dinner Dance

You have to be a good dancer to make it as a honeybee. Honeybees dance to send their messages. When a bee finds food, it flies back to the hive to dance. The type of dance it does tells the other bees where the food is.

If the food is far away, the bee's dance looks like the number eight. This dance is known as the "waggle dance." If the food is close to the hive, the bee dances in circles. And the more flowers there are with sweet, liquid **nectar** to feast on, the faster the dance!

THE HIVE JIVE
BULLETIN BOARD

Wanted:
Dancing Honeybee

The bee we are looking for:
- likes to travel and has a good sense of direction.
- loves nectar and pollen and knows where to find it.
- knows all the dance moves, such as Close-to-Home and Faraway.

Bees without rhythm need not apply.
Send applications to Queen Bee c/o The Hive.

Belinda has one pair of red dancing shoes for sale. Only worn once.

The Waggle Dance

Start

Waggly bit

Around the outside

Move in a figure eight.

For Their Ears Only

Elephants make several sounds that people can hear. But they also make **infrasonic** sounds that are too low for human ears to hear. If you see the skin on an elephant's brow flutter, you'll know it's making these secret sounds.

These infrasonic sounds can travel up to 10 kilometers (6 miles). They help elephants keep track of each other when the herd is spread out over a large area. If a baby elephant gets lost and calls out, the elephant rescue team sends it infrasonic rumbles to make the baby feel better until they arrive!

Ring, ring!

Hello!

Q: How do elephants speak to each other?

A: On 'elephones!

27

Face It!

Chimpanzee faces look a lot like human faces. Like us, they can use their faces to show how they are feeling. You'll be amazed how much chimp speak you already understand. What do you think these chimps are feeling?

So now you know what animals **are** really **saying.**

Answers

Face 1
When chimps are angry, they open their mouths wide and shout. They frown and their eyes get smaller, just like ours do. They can also make their hair stand on end.

Face 2
When chimps are bored, they look a lot like we do when we are bored.

Face 3
When chimps are happy and feeling playful, they make laughing noises. Their eyes get wider and they show their teeth. It's a chimp grin!

Face 4
When chimps are surprised and interested, they open their eyes wide and drop their mouths a little, like we do.

Fact File

Ever notice how high a dog lifts its leg when leaving its scent on a tree? That's because it wants other dogs to think that a really TALL dog was there first.

In ancient Egypt, you could be put to death if you killed a cat. And dead cats were often buried as mummies.

How cool is this?

STOP STOMPING! My knees need some peace!

An ant's knees pick up sound waves. It hears with its knees!

A chimpanzee called Panbanisha uses a keyboard with symbols for words. She has a vocabulary of about 3,000 words.

Glossary

glands body parts that prepare a substance to be given off or to be used by the body

infrasonic a sound with a frequency too low for humans to hear

instinct a response or ability that an animal is born with

muzzle the part of an animal's head that includes the jaws, mouth, and nose

nectar a sweet liquid made by plants that bees make into honey

pack a group of animals of the same kind

scents odors or smells that animals give off or leave behind

Index